Usborne
First Sticker Book
Feelings

Illustrated by Joanne Partis

Words by Holly Bathie and Alice Beecham

Designed by Meg Dobbie

You'll find all the stickers at the back of the book.

How do you feel?

You can often tell how people are feeling by the look on their face. Read the feelings labels, then stick the children's pictures in the right place to match how they are feeling.

Happy

Tired

Angry

Worried

How are you feeling today?

Add a face sticker here to show how you're feeling.

Add more children to this page, then stick on a face sticker to show how they feel.

Those were brand new!

I love my Dad.

I've lost my other glove.

You naughty dog!

My friends have come to play.

The dog ate all the cake.

I love this story.

Playtime feelings

Some children find rides and slides exciting, and some find them a bit scary. However you feel is OK. Stick on lots of children and how they are feeling.

Sick

Cheerful

5

At a fun run

Stick on the children taking part in the fun run. How are they all feeling? Add more friends and family cheering them on.

Jealous

2

1

3

Body feelings

When you feel hungry or cold, your body is giving you a clue about what it needs. Can you add all the stickers to the page?

My tummy is making noises.

My head aches and my mouth feels dry.

I feel all sweaty and dizzy.

You might be **hungry**, and need to eat something.

You might be **thirsty**, and need to drink something.

You might be **hot**, and need to take off your coat.

I'm shivering.

I think I'm going to be sick.

I can't stop yawning!

You might be **cold**, and need to put on some warm clothes.

You might be **unwell**, and need to tell a grown-up.

You might be **tired**, and need to have a rest.

There are lots of other ways your body can show your feelings.

If you are **excited** or **nervous**, you might feel like you have **butterflies in your tummy**.

If you are **angry** or **embarrassed**, you might feel **hot and sweaty**.

If you **have a shock** or are **frightened**, you might feel **out of breath**.

Away from home

These children are camping in the woods and exploring nature. Add all the stickers to show how they are feeling. Stick on a friend for someone who is feeling lonely.

At a birthday party

You might feel all sorts of things at a birthday party, such as cheerful, shy or frustrated. Add children with all of these feelings to the scene.

HAPPY BIRTHDAY!

Oh dear!

Shy

Pin the tail on the donkey.

What to do about feelings

Everyone has difficult feelings sometimes, and there are things you can do to make yourself feel better.
Add all the stickers to these pages.

If you feel angry, you could bang a drum very loudly.

If you feel sad, do something nice for someone else.

You're my best friend.

If you're worried or sad, hugging someone can cheer you up.

Talking to someone about your worries can make you feel better.

Here are some things you can do to help you feel calmer and happier.

This is my happy place.

Find a quiet place to snuggle up and calm down.

Close your eyes and breathe in and out slowly and deeply.

Do something you enjoy, such as reading a book that you like.

Spend time playing with your friends.

At bedtime

It's the end of a busy day. Stick on children feeling relaxed, sleepy and loved as they listen to a bedtime story.

How do you feel? pages 2-3

Choose one of these face stickers to show how you're feeling.

Furious	Excited	Sad	Calm	Worried

Bored	Surprised	Sleepy	Angry	Happy